Collection
Entreprises et société
sous la direction de Bernard Deforge
et Laurent Acharian

TO SERVE AND TO GROW

PIERRE BELLON

TO SERVE AND TO GROW
The iconoclastic beliefs
of Sodexo's founder

With the collaboration of Bruno Dranesas

*Translated from the French
by Lindsay Lightfoot*

PARIS

MANITOBA

2019

© *2019, Société d'édition Les Belles Lettres,
95, boulevard Raspail, 75006 Paris.*

ISBN : 978-2-37615-072-5

Translator's Note: All citations from books and articles in this text have been translated from the original French or from a French translation of the original.

PREAMBLE

This book was conceived and written based on a series of conversations with Pierre Bellon. It tells us about his life and his convictions. It is the portrait of a great French business leader, founder of *Sodexo*, a campaigning entrepreneur and believer in human development. He is an exceptional man with an unusual story. We hear from Pierre Bellon, but in addition, his trenchant observations are set within an overall context by different experts and commentators who shed light on events, echoing his own account. We hope to create not just a memoir but to hand on his experience as well.

INTRODUCTION

REVOLUTIONARY

The scene took place in early 2014, during a dinner-debate in which Pierre Bellon was participating. That evening, he challenged the Minister for Labor, Michel Sapin, on the fact that many French entrepreneurs were leaving France to settle abroad.

"How will you prevent entrepreneurs, attracted by a more favorable economic, tax and social environment, from leaving for Britain, Switzerland, Australia or Singapore to develop their businesses, handicapped as they are here by an over restrictive labor code?"

Rather than replying directly, the politician, a member of Jean-Marc Ayrault's government, under the Hollande presidency, turned towards the guests around him and asked them, *"Who is this guy?"*

Pierre Bellon's reaction?

"I was stunned when I heard that."

Because by then, Pierre Bellon had long since been the embodiment of one of France's most successful and best-known companies, of which he was the founder. This was *Sodexo*, and at 89 years old he is still their Honorary Chairman. To correct this blunder alone is sufficient reason to make the story of this little-known but major business leader available to the general public. However, it is not the most important motivation for writing this book.

It is worth listening to Pierre Bellon, because this man, one of most powerful captains of industry in France, asks the same question about the current situation as many anxious citizens.

"How do we reintroduce morals into capitalism? That is what we need today. If we have people in yellow vests it's because there's a problem, don't you think?"

When he says this, Pierre Bellon does not aim to come across as a leftwing business leader. He believes it is not up to the law to shape companies. It is for business leaders to recognize their responsibilities and to act accordingly.

"Is it revolutionary to say that I founded my company to create jobs? If that's revolutionary, then yes, I'm a revolutionary boss."

How does one become a revolutionary boss? What paves the way for this? Which values? Which grievances? What makes you different from anyone else? These are the important questions behind this book. Essential questions, at a time when endless scandals regularly sully the image of founders and CEOs, and consumers and the public expect an increasingly strong social engagement from companies.

In the spring of 2019, in the space of just ten days, the press headlines dwelt on two controversial affairs. The first concerned the exorbitant exit package (€14 billion) paid to the Executive Chairman of *TechnipFMC*, Thierry Pilenko, even though the oil engineering company was in the red – "*a bonus for failure*" commented Geoffroy Roux de Bézieux, president of the *Medef* (*Mouvement des Entreprises de France* –the national federation of French employers). The second polemic centered around the astronomical golden parachute promised to Tom

Enders, the German *Airbus* CEO, on leaving his job – €37 million, according to calculations made by French corporate governance analysts, *Proxinvest*, when the European manufacturer was rocked by an anticorruption investigation.

With such practices, it's unsurprising that public opinion is fired up and that there have been smear campaigns attacking questionable business practices. In 2018, 95% of companies saw their reputation decline in comparison to the previous year.

"It is not in the least surprising that the difference in wage levels between bosses and the remainder of the company is unacceptable in the view of public opinion. Indeed, this disparity in treatment is truly shocking, especially since the bosses have guaranteed pensions, unrelated to their performance. As regards myself, I have always taken great care to be beyond reproach in the matter of payment. Today, as Honorary Chairman of Sodexo, *I have opted to receive no salary. I receive dividends as a shareholder."*

Over recent years it is no exaggeration to say that a deep sense of mistrust has set in.

"It is certain that the CAC 40 companies must have a social and community minded

conscience. The time when a chairman was judged solely on his financial and stock exchange performance is over," declared Vincent de la Vaissière, when the 8th study by his *VcomV* consultancy on the communication modes of major business leaders in the CAC 40 was published.

The time has come for responsible corporate governance. According to a study by *Accenture*, 56% of French consumers want companies to take a stand on social and environmental values. 60% favor companies which communicate their commitment actively. And 66% affirm that their decisions on purchases are influenced by the values and actions of business leaders. They also indicate a preference for those prioritizing quality ingredients (80%), fair treatment for employees (64%) and respect for the environment (62%). We are currently at a point when companies must change, under pressure from consumers and the general public who wish to see greater fairness, improved ethics, quality products and Services and companies making a positive impact on society.

In this context, Pierre Bellon's words, based on his highly individual experience and an unrelenting sense of indignation, are invaluable in shedding light on the current debate. A humanistic, social and community minded business leader. It is this commitment in favor of human development which leads to the epithet 'revolutionary.' When you ask where his rectitude comes from, he replies, "*from my father.*"

The account of his life is an antidote to cynicism and pessimism. This book addresses all those who think, like him, that history is never written in advance. And that the best way of advancing, of progressing, is through enterprise.

CHAPTER 1

EMPLOYMENT

If you have not met Pierre Bellon, just think of this number - 460,000. It is the number of employees at *Sodexo* (as of August 31, 2018), the company that this captain of industry created from zero in 1966, and which within half a century has become the largest French employer in the world. Considering this achievement alone, it is tempting to write a book crammed with adjectives and superlatives to relate this extraordinary story. But at 89 years old, still seated at his desk at 255, quai de la Bataille de Stalingrad, the registered office of *Sodexo* in Issy-les-Moulineaux, Pierre Bellon does not want a sycophantic portrayal of his journey through life.

"Talking about myself worries me."

And to make clear his aversion to seeking the limelight, he shows me Helene

Vacchiali's book, sitting on his desk '*Moi, moi et moi*' ('Me, me and me'), published in 2017, a study of narcissism.

"*Renown has always worried me. I've seen so many powerful men let themselves be seduced by the glamour of the media and become monsters of pride, no longer listening to their voters, their consumers, their clients or their staff, convinced that they were always right. Me, me and me, that's what kills companies, associations and organizations.*"

Let's be clear. This book was not Pierre Bellon's idea.

"*I was against it,*" he told me.

In 2005, at the time of *Sodexo*'s 40th anniversary, a book was produced recounting the company's history, but the CEO and founder preferred a general account in which he did not figure very much, giving star billing to the executives' and employees' roles during the most important episodes in company history. The title "*I've had a lot of fun*" was chosen to avoid the cult of the ego and appearing swollen headed. It is the boss's warning to his teams. We mustn't take ourselves too seriously or get puffed up with pride.

"The very nature of the company is humility in the face of the facts. If by simply doing all that we had fun, that's not too bad, is it?"

Let's take Pierre Bellon at his word and stick to the facts. In 2018, *Sodexo* was the world leader for Quality of Life services, established in 72 countries, and a sales turnover of more than €20 billion—with 43% realized in North America, 39% in Europe (13% in France) and 18% in the rest of the world, as of August 31, 2018. The group works in companies, schools, hospitals, the army, communities and prisons. With a hundred professions and trades across the world: catering, maintenance, security, reception, cleaning, mail etc. Serving 100 million consumers every day!

"Fifty years ago, when I made it Sodexo's *mission to improve the Quality of Life of its employees and of all those we serve, while contributing to the economic, social and environmental development of the cities, regions and countries we work in, I think we were ahead of the times."*

Taking this impressive development into account, any normally curious economic journalist and observer interested in the life of companies would want to ask Pierre Bellon how it all came about. I was at last able to put some questions to him, and to discuss his ideas and learn about his engagement, the day he finally agreed to listen to his family and friends.

"More and more frequently they said—your life, all that you've done with Sodexo—*here's an opportunity to talk about your management principles, to explain your belief in human development, to share your strategy of independence for the company, to give your opinion of capitalism, to speak about your engagements as an employer, to stress the importance of service, to have a go at technocracy, to speak for the intra-entrepreneur, to talk about the creation of the* Association pour le Progrès et le Management *(APM—the* Sodexo Management Institute*). Obviously, all these subjects are very close to my heart. They are fundamentally important. It has made me think things through. I cannot deny that I am a public figure. Today, I am Honorary Chairman of* Sodexo *and my daughter Sophie chairs the board of directors with Denis Machuel as CEO. It's certainly time to tell people about my battles and my beliefs."*

One particular fact is key to Pierre Bellon's unique career—he "envisaged" his company before founding it. In the book "*I've had a lot of fun*," Jean Frégnac, adviser to the founder of *Sodexo* from the outset, recalled how Bellon had laid out for him the company philosophy, its purpose and its general objectives, in great detail. Reminded of this, Pierre Bellon thought back to the vision he had set out from the beginning.

"In France in the 1960s, Marxist thinking was still very widespread, private companies were mistrusted and, before creating Sodexo, *I asked myself why I wanted to start a company? My answers were the fundamental basis of our philosophy, then and now. A company is its clients; a company is the women and men who work there; a company is its shareholders who provide financial resources. I told myself that to create a company is to try to meet the needs of the clients, the needs of the workforce and the needs of the shareholders. But I very quickly realized that it was not easy to satisfy the clients, the workforce and the shareholders all at once. And the only way I found to satisfy these conflicting interests, was through growth. Of course, I only*

thought of organic growth. And so, crazily, the philosophy of the company even before we started was that my company would be a company of growth."

Who, then, is *Sodexo*'s founder? In an article entitled '*The Bellons*,' published by *L'Express* on June 26, 2002, this sentence sums him up: "*The man is natural and straightforward. A quasi-miracle. 'I get on with things and I observe myself in the process. I enjoy observing myself. That's why I'm relaxed, I stand back from events and I'm credited with a sense of humor by those who know me well'.*"

Above all, his life has been an adventure. He often employs the word '*buddies*' to talk about those in his circle. He is a man of passions—sport, travel and good food. During our talks, he frequently laughed, was irritated, angry, swore a bit and made outrageous remarks.

"*I was born in Marseilles, I'm from the south.*"

No matter what the subject, he is inexhaustible. He loves to talk. He's a storyteller. It is a real pleasure to listen to him talking about his life, so animated is he in his enjoyment. He laughs at himself. His acerbic humor is typically Provençal. There is often a twinkle in his eye. At 89 years old, his mind is still amazingly sharp, even if his body shows signs of fatigue and certain sentences are punctuated by long silences. When asked what he was like at work, he replies,

"I have a tremendous capacity for work. I'm an entrepreneur. I can't sit and be idle. I've been lucky in having an iron constitution. If I didn't work, I would die."

At the office, the boss was anything but easy, described as hard-headed, fiery, tough, irascible, interfering, methodical—meetings ended in the inevitable ritual *"what, with whom and when?"*

"A meeting is only useful if it solves a particular problem. The underlying idea should always be to find ways to remain more competitive than your competitors. This is why any meeting must have an agreed agenda. It is a question of defining properly what's on the table so as to avoid getting lost in pointless discussions. An important point—only competent people should attend—those directly concerned. If not, you soon realize that everyone is always in meetings, and the people in charge to whom you want to

speak, to get things done, are always unavailable. Which is completely counter-productive. That's why I insist on a questionnaire for each participant as a matter of course. What problem needs solving? What is your value-added? What decisions will you take? Who will implement them? When will these decisions be implemented? I applied this method everywhere that I was in charge. Every meeting should end with a report specifying the decisions taken and the next stages, setting out each participant's mission. If not, the meeting has no value. It is pointless. This way of proceeding made it possible to limit the length of meetings for many managers who therefore had more operational time, making them more efficient compared to our competitors."

"I'm often asked what I'm most proud of. I am proudest of having made it possible for many people to have grown with the company. My success lies in having created a company able to promote women and men and contribute to their personal fulfillment. I think that's my greatest achievement. Is it revolutionary to say that I created my company to create jobs?"

To create jobs. Pierre Bellon's drive was born out of trauma. In the mid-1960s, ship-building in Provence, the mainstay of regional industrial activity, began its inexorable decline to a slow death over a twenty-year period. To gauge the shock caused by the coming economic catastrophe, it is necessary to remember just how important the Ciotat shipyards had been since 1835, together with those of La Seyne-sur-Mer and Port-de-Bouc since 1836 and 1899. In addition, many men were employed in the three towns which developed around these sites. A new social model gradually arose with the arrival of this abundant labor force and the opening of small businesses. At their peak, these three Provençal shipyards employed 13,800 workers and generated nearly 25,000 jobs, while launching more than 1,000 large ships.

But from the start of the 1950s, the first signs of crisis began to appear. Commissions from the Merchant Navy Ministry, previously funded by war reparations, ended and foreign competition began to emerge, particularly from the British—20-30% cheaper—and finally, public subsidies were reduced. With decolonization and the rise in air transport, the reorganization of the shipbuilding sector became inevitable. In 1965, La Seyne ended the year with a record deficit involving the loss of more than 500 jobs. The company was forced into a change of ownership. But worse was to come a hundred kilometers away in Port-de-Bouc. In 1964, the order books were empty. 900 workers were laid off, in spite of strikes and popular protests. In 1966, the *Chantiers et Ateliers de Provence* went bankrupt. The last ship under construction, the Provence, was towed to the Ciotat shipyard.

"Seeing the shipyards, world leaders, suddenly disappear, made me think. I was very afraid of recession, dismissal and unemployment."

If Pierre Bellon was deeply marked by this economic and social tragedy which saw the collapse of shipbuilding in Provence, it was not solely because he witnessed these events up close, living in the port city of Marseilles. If he reacted so intensely, it was because ships had been part of his family environment since birth. In 1892, his grandfather Joseph-Baptiste started a company to supply boats.

"He was bad tempered. A difficult man. He became an entrepreneur a little by chance. He was employed as a clerk and then in accounts at

Gaymard's, *a company that supplied food to ferries and cargo liners from the* Compagnie de Navigation Paquet. *They ran the first regular shipping line between Marseilles and Morocco. His life changed the day his boss asked him to deal with a new customer, the* Compagnie de Navigation Mixte, *whose activities covered freight and passenger transport to Algeria and Tunisia. Frederic Gaymard told my grandfather he had a businessman's head. This was his chance. This business was right for him. He said he was recommending him to the* Compagnie de Navigation Mixte. *When you see the phenomenal competition between companies in today's world, this helping hand was extraordinary. Later, my father Félix joined the company, aged 18. When my grandfather died, he took over, with his brother Fernand. I joined in 1958, after obtaining my diploma from* HEC *Business School in Paris and completing my military service as a naval officer."*

Pierre Bellon was perfectly placed to watch the tragic destiny of the shipyards.

"One of my strengths is observation and an ability to grasp the facts and understand what is going to happen. It has been a deciding factor in my life."

Seeing his world falling to pieces, Pierre Bellon very quickly realized he would need to change careers. The time when the port of Marseilles supplied the large steamers which had been the pride of pre-war colonial France, was now past.

"It was a time of new beginnings. One world had ended. Another was being born," according to Claude Weill, in a special edition about the Sixties of the *Nouvel Observateur*, December 21, 2011.

Pierre Bellon was trying to find his way. The idea of setting up on his own account began to form at a time when the sacrosanct lunchbreak of French employees started to be eroded. Transport time between work and home was increasing and employees returned home less often, grabbing sandwiches or other French-style fast-food on the run. The entry of women in the labor market also constituted a small revolution which made long lunch breaks at home with cheese and dessert less automatic. Thereafter, employees needed to be able to eat quickly and inexpensively. In tune with his times, Pierre Bellon followed the trend with a plan to feed employees on the spot, in their workplace. It was not his idea. Others had already started out, like Jacques Borel, a pioneer as early as 1959.

"It must be admitted, he had phenomenal courage. Even if we were rivals and even if I was far from sharing all his ideas."

In fact, in Marseilles, the *SHRM* (*Société Hôtelière et de Ravitaillement Maritime*) were the first to launch in this new venture.

"They were our largest competitor, a true empire in the food supply sector, infinitely more powerful than us. The company supplied, for example, the ships of the Compagnie des Messageries Maritimes et de la Compagnie Générale Transatlantiques. *Compared to them, founded in 1902 by Joseph Calizi and Louis Altieri, we were pathetic, it has to be said. So, when I discovered in 1962 that* SHRM *were launching* Télérestor, *soon renamed* SHR *(*Société Hôtelière de Restauration*), to deliver cooked meals to companies in Marseilles, my first reaction was that it would take a lot of nerve to try and compete with them. But above all, I had to decide quickly. Would I follow suit or not? Remember how things were in the 60s. I had a hunch that the mass catering market*

would develop hugely. I was not sure, but I had this hunch. I had understood that businesses wanted to get rid of this service. So, I was very tempted to move into the meal delivery business, but I was still a bit hesitant. Why? Because at the time, in France, the image of this business was very poor, and the quality was equally so. Finally, I decided to go into it, but with a single clear idea. I would improve the quality of meals served in the workplace. This objective has not altered one iota in 50 years. The client and the consumer are king. They are our living."

At the end of 1962, Pierre Bellon took his first sidestep with the family business. It was still a food supply business, but instead of ships, they now sold to companies. To succeed, he called on the services of a pal from *HEC*, Rémi Baudin, his first associate who would thereafter play an important role in *Sodexo*.

"I needed a free hand to prepare setting up the business. So Rémi took care of managing the maritime business. I'd lost touch with him, but then I bumped into him in Orly airport when he was flying to Greece and me, to the Middle East. He was working in consultancy and told me he

didn't want to stay in it forever. A few weeks later I asked him to come and work for me. That was the beginning of it all.

My uncle Fernand lent me his warehouse, a very small space of 50m² in his anchovy factory. I hired a van and bought a stove. Then I took on a driver and a cook, and I started to deliver meals to companies. I produced up to 700 meals a day. I was happy. But the traffic in Marseilles was terrible and the insulated delivery containers weren't very good – the chips went soft and the steaks were overcooked. So very soon the orders started to drop off because people weren't getting the service they wanted. That's when I realized this wasn't the way to do it. I understood then that what was needed was to set up directly in our clients' premises.

That was a big step, because I hadn't any money. Clients allowed me to use their facilities, so I didn't have to invest in premises or in very expensive equipment. Our major costs were the raw materials and salaries. I quickly realized that margins are tight in this line of business so there was no room for mistakes. A cent is a cent. Everything counts. There's a reason I often call us penny pinchers."

Pierre Bellon had made his decision. His future would lie in company catering. As a clincher he needed to win his first contract, both to confirm his gut feeling and to give himself the means to achieve his ambition.

"I nearly died" he exaggerated, boasting about the risk he took.

It all began one fine evening in 1964. It was a beautiful night. The *HEC* alumni in Marseille were holding one of their regular get togethers. Pierre Bellon was there.

"In the course of a conversation, I heard one of the others, who worked for SHR, *say that they'd just replied to a tender from the* Atomic Energy Commission *(*AEC*) to manage a new cafeteria at their center in Pierrelatte, in the Drôme. It was a big deal. I knew immediately that I had to go up against them."*

The next day he went along to *AEC*, where he met their senior purchasing and catering managers who told him the tender was closed. But Pierre Bellon managed to persuade them to extend the tender window by a fortnight, which would give him time to prepare his proposal. That started the race against the clock, and a huge challenge.

Starting from scratch, with no experience and no business references, a self-service canteen for 2,000 people with new equipment. He faced competition from the big hitters in the field – *SHR* and *Jacques Borel*, both much larger companies. On paper his chances looked slim. But his audacity would pay off.

"It was a huge leap, more or less in the dark. I was taking an enormous risk. I realized that I was barely credible. I had to inspire the decision makers at AEC *with confidence. That's why I told them I was going to hire staff in advance so that if I won the contract, we'd be ready to start at once and sure of a good launch. So, I quickly hired chefs and cashiers – and I got* Sud Aviation *at Marignane, a big helicopter manufacturer in the region, to agree to train them on the job in their self-service. It was off the wall. At the time,* Sud Aviation *didn't use subcontractors, so its employees' food service was not outsourced. Yet the directors agreed to open their doors to us so that I could train and coach my team with their facilities. Think what that meant for a small, almost non-existent outfit like mine. But I bluffed my way through. I kept my*

promise and had people ready to start immediately. I polished the proposal and I was very aggressive on pricing as well as totally transparent. They liked that a lot."

If the challenge seemed almost insurmountable at the outset, he pulled it off. Pierre Bellon won an unlikely victory, watched dumbfounded by the losers, who couldn't believe their eyes.

"When AEC *told me that it was the first time one of their restaurant launches had gone so well, I was able to renegotiate the initial prices, which were unsustainable. I had resigned myself to an initial loss because it was such a great opportunity. I put a team of seventy people on site. But I warned my client that because of the monthly losses, I wouldn't last more than six months. So, I went to see two of their directors in their Paris office. We spent an hour together. At the end of that time I told them that that hour had cost* AEC *a lot more than the increase I was seeking. They couldn't help laughing and told me I was right. From then on, prices were agreed on each site and not centrally. And my problem was solved."*

His success with *AEC* confirmed Pierre Bellon in his drive to have his own company.

And after Pierrelatte, other contracts in the Marseille region followed.

"Those first commercial successes bore out what I had felt. The market potential was there. We just had to go for it."

The time had come to tell his father that he wanted to start his own business.

"As I knew that what I had to say would hurt him, I hesitated a long time before talking to him. It must have been the end of 1964 or early 1965. I told him. I didn't believe in the future of shipping in Marseille any more. He was very dismayed. It had been his whole life. So, pointing out the decline and recession in the world he'd always known was hard to hear, but it was true. When my father asked me why I wanted to start my own business I told him I needed to be independent. But the real difficulty came when I told him I wanted my company to have my name. He said I was mad. If I went bankrupt, it would damage the whole family and the reputation they'd worked for. My father was quite well-known. I didn't want to go against him on this. In the group, even though it was small, we had companies whose names were respected, such as the SOciété D'Exploitations

HÔtelières Maritimes, A*ériennes* et Terres-tres *(Company for Hotelier Operations on Land, Sea and Air). So, I decided to shorten this to Sodexho (which later will become* Sodexo*). My father gave me his blessing but imposed one condition—we had to split the equity between my two sisters, my brother and me—25% each. I was against it, naturally. I refused the condition and won the argument, beginning with the majority shareholding, having my sisters Annie and Michelle and my brother Bernard as minority shareholders who agreed not to interfere directly with the company's management. It was essential to keep the company's organigram and my family tree separate."*

On March 9, 1966, Pierre Bellon officially launched his business. And he promised himself that day that it would always have sustained growth and avoid the fate of the naval shipyards that had marked him so deeply over the preceding years.

"First and foremost, I had to be in a growth sector. I couldn't see myself laying off masses of people."

CHAPTER 2

GROWTH

Answering the question, how does an SME in Marseille become an international enterprise, employing 460,000 people worldwide, Pierre Bellon replied,

"Before you can grow, you have to begin small. That's my philosophy in a nutshell. It's a long road to success. To be an entrepreneur, you need dreams, and you must try to realize them without falling flat on your face. I've always been drawn to the open sea, to limitless horizons. You know, when you climb to the top of the Notre-Dame de la Garde basilica, in fine weather, you can see right across Marseilles, its harbor and the Mediterranean Sea. This unbeatable view has definitely had a big influence on my wish to build a global business one day."

Pierre Bellon was 36 years old when he launched his business. He was born in

Marseilles on January 24, 1930, the second child in a family of four. He has two sisters; Annie is two years older and Michelle two years younger than him. Bernard, the youngest, is five years his junior. His childhood passed quietly and in fairly comfortable circumstances, until the premature death of his mother, Claire, when he was twelve years old.

"I didn't really know her. I suffered a lot. She had cancer so she had several operations. Each time she went in for an operation, she left us letters because she thought she was going to die. In her final letter she told Annie to look after our sister Michelle. To me she said that I must look after our brother Bernard. And she told the four of us to all look after our father. You know, that sort of responsibility makes you grow up fast. My mother's death was a great sorrow which has lasted throughout my life. You are what you are, perhaps through your own personality, but also thanks to the people you meet and the events that you live through in the course of your existence."

To get over this terrible loss, this bottomless void, the family came together to support and help each other. Pierre, his two sisters, his brother and his father.

"He brought us up. He never remarried. He was the cement that bound the family together. We were in awe of him. He was an entrepreneur who was very involved in the employers' association, at a local level, especially within the Fédération des Associations régionales du Centre National du Patronat français *(The French employer's association known as the* CNPF, *later the* Medef—Mouvement des Entreprises de France). *He was also one of the founders of the Family Allowance Fund. When he died, I had numerous letters from union delegates praising his ability to dialogue."*

In Marseilles, Pierre Bellon attended a school run by the Jesuits, the Provence School. *"A rigorous and disciplined school but a happy one."*

Aged eleven, he broadened his education by joining the scouts.

"I was a patrol leader of the Wolves whose rallying cry was 'Wolves forever.' Then I became patrol leader of the Swallows and there our rallying cry was 'Swallows as swift as they come.' After we'd been there a few years, the troop leader organized the totem ceremony for us. A totem is an animal name and adjective that is

chosen for the scout and corresponds to how others see them, according to physical character-istics and also behavior. It underlines their personal values. My Totem was 'faithful dolphin,' of which I am very proud, because the dolphin's characteristics are to have fun in the water and be loyal, and I simply can't stand disloyalty. Along with this real Totem, between ourselves we gave each other joke Totems. Among which I remember 'independent bulldog,' but especially 'likes a dialogue where he's the only one talking,' which I didn't like at all. But I must admit that this second joke Totem served me well in life because I realized that there was a good bit of truth in it and so I tried to correct this aspect of my character. This is why I still have a sheet of paper in my desk drawer, which says 'Shut up and listen.' And I bring it out during meetings to stop me from replicating the joke Totem. The scouts were very important to me, I can tell you. I liked it because you devel-oped as a person and learnt initiative. They gave me my first experience of management. That's where I got my leadership training. That's where I learned that a group is more about team

strength than one man's drive. And I also real-
ized that some people are natural leaders by
temperament, and others natural followers."

In November 1942, German troops
crossed the demarcation line and Marseilles
was occupied by the 244th Infantry Division
under General Hans Schaefer. The Second
World War had come to Pierre Bellon's
hometown. Other than at the start of the
conflict, before the armistice was signed in
June 1940, they had not been directly
involved in operations, except for a few
bombardments.

"The day when I really experienced war at
first hand was May 27, 1944. That day, the
Americans bombarded the city."

The account of this day that deeply trau-
matized the local people, is retold in the
newspaper *La Provence*, in an article on May
25, 2017.

"For a long time, the focus has been the
Normandy landings and the fate of the large
ports on the Atlantic and Channel coasts. The
official history of the Second World war has
often tended to overlook the fact that Marseilles
was one of the principal cities to suffer badly in

this conflict. Already ravaged by the raids and destruction of the districts around the Old Port, the city of Marseilles underwent, in particular on May 27, 1944, one of the most fatal bombardments in France. In a few minutes, 130 'flying fortresses,' American Boeing B-17s coming from Italy, dropped nearly 800 bombs of 250 and 500 kg, or nearly 300 tons of munitions and almost as many explosives on the city. The effect on the ground was devastating. More than 400 buildings were flattened, reduced to the state of rubble, and nearly 850 others rendered completely uninhabitable. The damage was such that about fifty fires were started across the city, complicating the task of rescuers, also confronted with cuts in water supply. As for the cost in lives, it was terrible: 1,750 Marseillais died in the storm of bombs and fire; a great number of them killed by the blast. 2,760 people were wounded, generally seriously."

Less well known than June 6, the allied landings in Provence began on August 15. Their objective was to destroy the coastal fortifications of the Mediterranean Wall, to the south of the Atlantic Wall, established by Erwin Rommel, often called the 'Desert Fox,'

one the best-known German commanders of
the Second World War. Marseilles was, with
Toulon, the theatre of the hardest battles in
this campaign. Because the German garri-
sons, ordered to resist to the last, were
supported by a network of formidable gun
batteries and fortifications. The suburbs of
Marseilles were reached on August 22. But
General Schaeffer refused to surrender. On
August 25, the French Army launched an
attack on the Basilica of Notre-Dame-de-la-
garde. But they had to wait for support from
the American bombers from Italy before the
German guns on the islands of Friuli were
silenced on August 26. Marseilles was finally
liberated two days later.

After the end of the Second World War,
Pierre Bellon make two attempts to pass his
baccalauréat. In 1945, he failed his exam
"because of German," and to avoid a second
failure, he left his native city for Lyon and
passed his Elementary Math in June 1946
and his *baccalauréat* two months later.

*"In Marseilles, the temptations were too great
to work seriously."*

With his diploma in his pocket, he had a single objective—to go to the Parisian business school, *HEC*.

"I thought that it was the best school."

He went up to Paris and enrolled in the two years of classes in preparation for the entrance exam, known as *prépa*. Except, his first attempt was a fiasco and it took him four attempts in all to pass the entrance examination.

"It was a catastrophe. Because it was, I admit, very unusual to fail so many times, but I was very nervous in the exams and useless at foreign languages."

During his years in Paris before obtaining his diploma in 1954, this student clearly preferred practice to theory.

"I was interested in geography, history, economics, and law, but accountancy bored me. On the other hand, I loved sport and the students' union, of which I was a vice-president. When I was young, I did not read very much."

His only regret is not to have been on the first football team in *HEC*, having to make do, playing in the second team.

"I played in Lionel Messi's position," (the Argentinian magician crowned five times with the *Ballon d'Or*).

"I was number ten. When I shot with the ball, my foot hurt but as I was small and sturdy, when I got through the defense I would score. I loved it, tennis too, and action in general. I am not an intellectual."

Boosted by this experience, Pierre Bellon did his military service in the Navy, at a time when France, in the mid-1950s, was going through a difficult, tense and violent period of decolonization. On the other side of the Mediterranean from Marseilles, North Africa was in a constant state of upheaval emancipating itself from French rule. Tunisia and Morocco obtained their independence in 1956 but the war in Algeria intensified until the Evian Accords in 1962. In this climate of tension, Pierre Bellon was first posted to a submarine hunter. His next posting took him to the area of Kabylie in eastern Algeria, for maritime surveillance in support of ground troops. He was then sent to Egypt, where the situation was deteriorating following the nationalization of the Suez Canal by Nasser.

"In 1956, I found myself in the middle of the Suez expedition aboard the escort destroyer F722, 'Le Soudanais.'"

The French, British and Israelis were about to force Nasser to back down, but just as the finishing stroke was imminent, the Americans and Soviets insisted on a withdrawal of the Suez expedition, at midnight on November 6, 1956. This cease-fire was a diplomatic triumph for Nasser, whereas for the two European powers, it represented a serious loss of status. It was at this point that the USSR and the United States in particular, took their places on the Middle Eastern stage.

"If those two superpowers had not intervened, Nasser would have capitulated, because we were just one hour from Cairo at the time. We were on course for war. During this critical period, everybody's true nature came to the surface. I saw that not all men were equal when confronted by danger and fear. I saw strapping men who had the jitters, small men who made a stand with coolness and courage. Inevitably, that leaves its mark."

This naval training had a great effect on Pierre Bellon's life, his personality, his capacity to launch himself into a wide world without borders, on the vision behind his plans to develop *Sodexo* internationally, when the time came. He is proud to have been in the Navy, less familiar to the general public, more esoteric than the Army. He is inexhaustible on its history, whether to evoke its origins, the influence of Napoleon or the traumas of the Second World War such as the scuttling of the French fleet in November 1942 off Toulon, to evade the German army which had just captured the port. Or again, the dramatic episode of Mers-el-Kébir in July 1940 which saw the British attack the French fleet in Algeria, sheltered in the naval dock in the gulf of Oran, to prevent it falling into German hands. Or, again in 1940, the fate of the French Eastern Mediterranean fleet, called Force X, based in Alexandria in Egypt, forced to surrender to the British to avoid being scuttled.

After thirty-one months spent in the Navy, Pierre Bellon returned to land. He followed in his father's footsteps. Not only did he join the family company, but like him, he had a taste for engagement. He joined the Marseilles chapter of the *CJP* (Center for Young Employers)—an employers' movement which is happy to be known as 'the thorn in the side' of the senior organization, the *CNPF*, and which brings together young executives motivated by the conviction that companies can serve mankind.

"It was one of my friends, who employed 1,000 people, who introduced me to the CJP, although at the time I employed only four. Obviously, I was proud that an employer from a large company was happy to work with me. When I knew him better, I realized that what he did as an executive was far from impossible. I said to myself that I could follow his example and also become the boss of a large company."

The *CJP* was created in 1938 by Jean Mersch, then 27 years old, with the objective, of dissociating himself from the tough image of bosses, strongly criticized when the Popular Front won in 1936, a period marked by spectacular social evolution: wage increases, recognition of trade-union freedom, creation of company delegates, and two weeks' paid-leave in particular, as well as the introduction of the 40-hour week instead of 48-hour and collective bargaining agreements. The foundation of the *CJP* was aimed at conciliation after an increase in resentment of employers who had not acted well during strikes in 1936 and the following years. It was hoped to initiate a much more socially conscious approach from employers.

"Economic growth is without value if it is not supported by an ethic which gives primacy to a humane purpose," wrote Jean Mersch, whose Christian humanism formed the bedrock of the *CJP*.

The values of the *CJP* were those of Pierre Bellon. He feared it might bore him. But he found it to be a formidable debating ground where experiences were shared.

"What united us was an unshakeable faith in mankind. This philosophy was pretty close to the Christian education that I had received. In 1965, the CJP *supported company unions in total opposition to the* CNPF. *I agreed, obviously. It was important to work towards a more humane and fair society. That was the whole point of us. Most of my ideas were inspired or consolidated by those I encountered and talked to*

within many working groups. My company would never have become what it is if I had not been in the CJP. *Because that's where I learned most. That's where I learned self-confidence too."*

The *CJP* in Marseilles was started in 1939, one year after its creation at national level, with Pierre Bellon's father among its founders. On the 80th anniversary of this employers' movement in April 2019, Pierre Bellon recorded a video to be shown at the ceremony. In this audio-visual document, he gives several examples of what the *CJP* working groups brought him.

"My first working group was devoted to a company boss's own work. A consultant had asked us to note down, over a six-month period, everything we did each day as executives of our companies. I was convinced that I was going to get a pat on the head because in six months I had done heaps of things. But it was just the opposite, I had the worst review of the group. Why? Because the consultant's aim was to make us aware that an executive must concentrate on the most important elements relating to their company and not spread themselves too thin,

as I had done. I must say, his comments made me think hard and I changed my approach. In a second working group devoted to the company's strengths and weaknesses, which included several executives from family companies, I heard many people say they found it difficult to express certain truths to their relatives. That was very enlightening because it was clear to me that family companies could be very effective, much more effective than those quoted on the stock exchange, but only insofar as the family was very united and therefore people could speak freely, and there was no problem over succession because it had been resolved."

Pierre Bellon underwent other formative training at this time: that of *Cadippe* (Action Committee for the Development of the Interest of People in the Progress of their company) which brought together heads of businesses, executives and trade unionists whose objective was to promote truly responsible and constructive social debate.

"This experience marked me for life, because my upbringing was middle-class and so I had preconceived ideas about certain social classes. What struck me, was that among the union

*representatives, there were some who wanted to
build the same society as me, that is a fairer,
more humane society, with equality between
women and men. But obviously our chosen
methods were completely different. And that,
that had an enormous influence on me. It taught
me to always respect the work of the trade unions
and to listen to them."*

So, this was the Pierre Bellon who
founded *Sodexo* in 1966. By then he had
been married for six years to Danielle
Touret, from a middle-class Marseilles
family. They had just had a third child, François-Xavier, who followed Sophie in 1961
and Nathalie in 1964 and was succeeded by
Astrid in 1969. The time had come to accel-
erate the development of his company at a
national level, by gradually extending its
activity to areas beyond Provence.

*"It was clear to me that the market was in
Paris. I applied what I called artichoke tactics to
hide my plans from my competitors. I picked off
small contracts the way you thin out the leaves of
an artichoke, without attracting too much atten-
tion. Until one day I was spotted because the
contracts were increasingly large. In 1968,*

French industry underwent an important change with the arrival of the large Thomson-CSF *group, as a result of the merger of the electronics* Thomson Group *with the* Compagnie Générale de Télégraphie sans fil *(*CSF*). This group was renamed* Thales *in 2000. The point of this story is that it was* Sodexo *who won the contract to manage all their restaurants. An enormous contract which put us under the spotlight. There could be no more artichoke tactics.*"

In the mid-60s, France was at a turning point in its history of space exploration and the very young company created by Pierre Bellon would play a role in it. Since 1958 and the return of General of Gaulle to power, the question of national independence lay at the heart of French politics. Space became an essential component of this ambition, at the point when Americans and Soviets were disputing world supremacy in this sphere. The National Center for Space Studies (*CNES*) was therefore created in 1961. They set up their first launch pad in Algeria. After Algerian independence, adfollowing a study of 14 potential sites, the government chose French Guiana, notably because of its proximity to the equator, a zone which made it possible to carry out the space missions under optimal conditions. In 1966, *CNES* launched a consultation over the food service for employees working on the construction site at the Kourou base.

"Sodexo *tendered for it, but we were outbid by the more powerful SHRM. To understand where we'd gone wrong, I went to meet General Robert Aubinière, first president of CNES, and one of the fathers of Concorde. It was a good thing I did because he told me that since we were interested in the Guyanese Space Center we should know that they would need a second service provider in Kourou and that it was essential that we respond to the new invitation to tender which he was launching. This one would relate to general services. He explained to me that he particularly wanted to set up a mini-market for all the personnel and their families living in Guiana. I was very flattered because General Aubinière was a man of great integrity, whose sole aim was the promotion of France. However, I had to tell him that we had never done that before, and that we could not tender because the response to the first invitation to*

*tender had already cost us a lot and we did not
have the financial means to sustain a second
failure. But he persuaded me to take the risk. To
meet the new requirements, I first asked my
father-in-law for help. He was a public works
contractor and vice-president of the Marseilles
Chamber of Commerce, and coincidentally he
was very familiar with the sector because the
region was just then planning to develop mini-
markets to extend the supermarket offer. So,
I invited my father-in-law to Guiana to draw up
the plans for a mini-market for me. Whereupon,
General Aubinière extended the specifications by
asking us to take care of cleaning, planting trees
and in particular, to oversee the start of security
services for CNES. So, then I found some
firemen from Paris, who have military status,
and invited them to come and work in Guiana.
Many of them were delighted with the opportunity. It was a great adventure for them. That's
how I met General Aubinière's specifications.
This enabled us to win the second invitation to
tender and immediately sign a contract which
guaranteed me a pre-tax income of 15% on all
our services. With this contract's backing I was
able to go to the Bank of Guiana and explain*

my situation. That I was committed to doing all this for CNES, but I had to warn them, I hadn't a cent. To which they responded, 'But Mr Bellon, that's not a problem, CNES backing is as solid as that of the French State. So, we will advance you all you need to launch your business in Guiana.' This victory was crucial because it gave us the means to diversify. Looking back, I now know that it was there that we inaugurated what was later called a multiservice offer, which consisted in widening our ability to supply our clients with all the services they required from us. Without CNES and the CEA, Sodexo would certainly not have become what it is today."

At the start of the 1970s, *Sodexo*'s development was mainly centered on France (catering for businesses as well as schools and hospitals etc.) However, they soon targeted Europe, and especially North Africa and the Middle East, following the oil trail, dotted with remote sites. These hotel-type facilities (food, lodging and laundry) were installed in remote areas close to large exploitation sites. Pierre Bellon had noticed the development of such sites from the end of the 50s, when doing business in the Sahara. Indeed, in 1958, the family company run by his father, had created, with two partners, a limited liability company in Algeria, the *Société Générale de Ravitaillement (SGR)*, which aimed to supply the French oil companies working there.

"*The situation was amusing. One of the two partners was in favor of hanging on to French Algeria and the other, called Raoul, supported the* Organisation de l'Armée Secrète *(*OAS – *a right-wing dissident paramilitary organization). Out of the three managers, at the age of 28, I was the one largely responsible for operations management. It didn't take me long to realize that our food stocks were disappearing mysteriously simply because Raoul was siphoning a lot off, unbeknown to us, for the OAS. You can imagine the next bit. This subsidiary company did not survive Algerian independence. The point is, that's how I got to know the region and have a ringside seat to observe the first remote site facilities for hydrocarbon exploration and the economic repercussions they were generating. This experience was invaluable to the growth of* Sodexo, *closely*

*linked at that time, to the massive oil field devel-
opments. Although everyone remembers that the
two oil crises in 1973 and 1979 shook the
majority of the world's economies, few people
remember what can only be called a veritable
black gold rush during this period. From the
Middle East to the North Sea, via Africa,
companies specializing in geological research,
drilling, production and refining, set up en masse
in these strategic zones, with exponential needs
for accommodation facilities and catering. In
spite of an extremely tense geopolitical context,
I decided to join the bandwagon on a large scale.
I went in against everyone's advice, in particular
the advice of the banks, who told me I was
completely insane. Actually, I've been very
careful in my investments, especially in Iran,
where I put in the minimum, on an assumption
which proved correct, that Khomeini would come
to power."*

The result was that in the 1980s, *Sodexo*
rose to be world number one in remote site
management and number one in the French
market of sub-contracted collective catering.
But the best was still to come. It was over the
following   decade   that   this   Marseilles

company metamorphosed to fulfil its outstanding destiny. With conquests on a global scale. The first phase commenced in 1995, at the point when Pierre Bellon went after a huge deal on the other side of the Channel, tackling a much larger company. For three years, he had had his eye on the British leader in collective catering—*Gardner Merchant*, the number one in Europe, a subsidiary of the British hotel chain, *Forte*.

"The clout of this British jewel was bound to increase our international standing."

The acquisition was made by amicable agreement. *Sodexo* doubled in size with 55,000 more employees.

"Gardner was a unique business. I couldn't afford to miss out on it. A business like that saved us six to seven years in the conquest of new market share."

After the conclusion of such a deal, Pierre Bellon might have had enough. Not a bit of it. Because he had an appointment with the world's largest market—the United States. A bridge too far? America, however, was already part of *Sodexo*'s history going back to the early 1970s, to be precise, to a phone call which started like a comedy sketch. Pierre Bellon remembers it well.

"I answered and I heard, 'Hello? Mister Bellon?' I was sure it was an American. He said, 'Here's the thing, I'm coming to Paris in a few days on my private plane. I would like to meet you because I am interested in your company.' I asked him who he was. He replied that his name was Bill Fishman and he was the president founder of ARA Services (which became Aramark in 1994), the world number one in collective catering. How had this American found us when we were really only a small company at the time? I understood that he wanted to buy us, but it was out of the question. I was determined to remain independent. However, I agreed to meet him to see who I was dealing with. I went to the United States with Remi Baudin to find out about ARA Services' methods. Bill Fishman showed us everything, absolutely everything, in an effort to convince me. In one sense it was a waste of time, but this trip to America saved me lots of time too. I was looking at a company 200 times larger than ours, already in divisions according to the type of

client—companies, defense, health establishments, retirement homes, catering and also facilities management. A unique experience. It was a shock. At the time, I had looked no further than Jacques Borel. *Suddenly, I saw that our trade was a global trade. Enough to make me dream of a global* Sodexo. *I understood that one day we'd need to launch on the American market even if it was dominated by two global giants,* Aramark *and* Marriott. *"*

From the middle of the 1980s, Pierre Bellon started to make small regional acquisitions in the United States, in a particular sector—catering and services in health and retirement establishments. In 1985 he made his first purchase on the East coast—*Seilers*—which made *Sodexo* the first French food services company to be established on the other side of the Atlantic. One year later, the group set up on the West coast with control of *Food Dimension Inc* (*FDI*), two acquisitions rapidly supplemented by three other local companies. But it was in 1997 that the presence of *Sodexo* in the United States saw a phenomenal acceleration.

"A young manager in the Société Générale *assured me that the* Marriott *hotel group would*

eventually sell its subsidiary company, Marriott Management Services *(*MMS*) to concentrate exclusively on its global hotel business. I didn't believe it."*

And yet this prediction would indeed prove correct. *Sodexo,* number four in the sector on the American market, was therefore a candidate for its purchase and approached *MMS,* number one in collective catering and food services in the United States. This gave rise to a new entity—*Sodexho Marriott Services (SMS).* At a single stroke, the French group acquired 100,000 new employees. This was Pierre Bellon's greatest coup by a long chalk.

"If I had consulted my lawyers, my bankers or experts in the United States, the deal would never have been done. I took the decision with the support of Edouard de Royère (former president of Air Liquide*), on the* Sodexo *board of directors, my wife and my children, who were shareholders, and with the agreement of the rest of the board. Considering the risk taken, I asked myself for years if it had been a good decision or not, and lost sleep over it for a long time. But I was borne out by what followed."*

After this Anglo-Saxon decade, the beginning of the 21st century would be marked by involvement in emergent countries with strong growth, in particular in Brazil, India and China. With one major characteristic of the group. Its development was achieved by multiplying the trades, as companies outsourced more and more functions. So much so that a number of them had no choice but to rely on an integrated supplier, or else having to coordinate the work of too many service providers. *Sodexo* established itself as an operator capable of taking care of all services, from the cafeteria to the ventilation system, including landscaping, reward programs and workforce benefits. In a little over fifty years, the specialist in food service supply had transformed itself into a facilitator of global solutions for its clients. The aim was to offer single management of all services including, of course, catering, but also, maintenance, security, reception, switchboard, cleaning, mail etc. All in all, more than one hundred fields of expertise. What a long way they had come since the *CNES* contract, which, on a small scale, started the multi-service offer that brought global success to *Sodexo*. And which now extends so far as to include services to private individuals, including childcare, concierge services and home help. Today, 'on-site services' account for 96% of sales turnover, realized mainly within company and administrative hubs, education, health and the seniors' sector. Alongside this major activity, the Benefits and Rewards Service accounts for the remaining 4%, with services to employees on the one hand and on the other through a diversification of services which includes in particular the programs of incentives and recognition.

"If people avail themselves of our entire offer, we are able to bring our Quality of life services to them from the nursery to the retirement home, throughout their working life, and their leisure. Isn't that wonderful?"

CHAPTER 3

PROMOTION

"I chose to go for organic growth from the start because it gives employees the chance to grow with the company through internal promotion. For me, helping people to succeed, is success in itself. In vain, my bankers would tell me that I was completely insane, that I was overstaffed. I would reply that motivating women and men was the only thing I knew how to do. For me, internal promotion was, and still is, the way to enable employees to flourish. And today it is still one of the strongest values of the Sodexo *brand as employer."*

In 2018, the level of engagement amongst employees in the group reached 69%, as against 59% in 2014 and 57% in 2012, the result of an evaluation carried out based on an anonymous questionnaire sent to employees.

"Our objective was to reach 65% because this is the level of staff engagement in the best

approved global companies. It is a cause of much satisfaction because that means that we are improving people's quality of life, within the company itself. This is absolutely vital. To be one of the companies most appreciated by its employees was a major ambition of ours for the group. I'm convinced that the success of the company depends on its employees' pride in belonging, their share in its values and on the improvement in their quality of life while at the service of our clients and of consumers. If I keep going to the staff canteen in Sodexo, *it is because that enables me to see whether people are happy or not. I'm very sensitive to atmosphere."*

Human resources are at the heart of the *Sodexo* project. How could it be otherwise when you've gone from anchovy warehouse in 1966 to multinational with 460,000 employees?

"When I started, our image was poor, and our line of business was looked down on. So, I tried to improve it by wagering everything on internal promotion within Sodexo. *Because the difficulty lay less in finding clients than in recruiting employees to honor our contracts.*

Here's a small anecdote—I often went on holiday to Club Med with my wife and my children, and it was there that I had the idea that the vocation of Sodexo *should be to improve the quality of life of the personnel and of everyone we serve. I had noticed that Club Med staff (known as GOs,* Gentils Organisateurs *meaning Kindly Organizers) were not very well paid. But the club's attraction for GOs lay elsewhere. There was a fun aspect. People were happy. The GOs were happy because they were liked and appreciated by the clients during evening entertainments. They were beautiful, danced well... As for Kind Members (holiday makers known as GMs), they sometimes even gave lessons in the activities. For example, I was a very good tennis player, so I gave lessons to the GMs. It was all very friendly, in a wonderful spirit of sharing.*

I was very impressed by that and it inspired me. Because in our trades, where wages are not high, it is essential to create an environment where the employees feel happy. 50 years on, the human dimension of our business is more crucial than ever. We calculate that our potential global development in 20 years' time will be 50 times our current sales turnover. This is the result of several broad trends: demographic trends with an increase in world population and life expectancy; the exponential outsourcing of services for companies and public administrations due to the constant increase in public deficits; the growing importance of the consumer's quest for wellbeing, an improved quality of life, better health and personalization of service; galloping urbanization with the development of megacities. All of these changes are favorable to Sodexo. *If we are to meet these steeply rising needs, most of our development depends on our human resources.*"

The company values, instilled in all the employees, are intangible, simple and comprehensible to everyone—the spirit of service, team spirit and the spirit of progress. And then there is the inevitable southern touch, the good humor that Pierre Bellon shares with the king of pastis, and that other large French family company born in the south of France. Pernod Ricard, whose slogan is "*Conviviality creators*," has become the world number two in the wines and spirits sector, headed up since 2015 by Alexandre Ricard.

"*I met Alexandre at a party, and he told me a story about his grandfather Paul Ricard,*

founder of the group, when he himself was still a
child. They were in a supermarket together and
his grandfather said to him: 'Look, you see, the
clients go and see the Ricard stand first of all.
You know why? Quite simply because the assist-
ants there smile much more than the others.'
I can completely identify with this anecdote
which is, truly, very important. It isn't
surprising that we are often thought alike. That's
the people of Provence, we are optimists. You
need to be an optimist to avoid being stressed."

In the blueprint for his organization Pierre
Bellon has always been haunted by one
particular pet hate, which has been with him
from the start of *Sodexo*—technocracy. The
word appalls him. For him, it's the worst
trap a company can fall into.

"Our size is our strength, but it is also our
greatest weakness. Becoming a technocracy is a
danger and it will kill the company spirit. In
1984, we numbered barely 8,000. Today we are
460,000. The risk has kept on growing. It's
become ever greater and ever more disturbing.

Especially now, with the digital tsunami,
the Big Data revolution and AI, the 'uberiza-
tion' of the business model and the growing

power of the consumer which is completely disrupting client relations and obliging large groups to reinvent themselves so as to stay in the race and make the most of all these disruptions which are changing the world at such a dizzying rate. In this context, requiring reactivity and agility, Pierre Bellon rails against the centralized and matrix organizations and says he has "*never had anything to do with them.*"

Why does it make Pierre Bellon so angry? We need to understand his aversion to any hierarchical or rigid system. The answer was in an interview given to *Les Echos* (a financial daily) on March 22, 2019 by the consultant Yves Morieux, director of Boston Consulting Group (BCG) Institute for Organization.

"Companies are adopting organizational matrixes which are increasingly complicated and, therefore, less and less effective. (…) If the matrix fosters co-operation within the company, which is essential in an increasingly complex economy, most companies do not know how to make this type of organization function. Too often, the matrix is added on to a hierarchical structure. This adds complication to complexity.

The result—a process which on average took three days now takes eight. Seven stages are still needed on average to sign off on a decision. Managers only add value 30% of their time. The remainder of the time, they are reporting on dozens of performance indicators. They manage the complexity, with planned tasks that make less and less sense. Companies have multiplied by six, on average, the number of indicators they use to evaluate their performance. So the system has become almost thirty-six times more complex (…) We still haven't devised an organizational model which makes it possible to get the best from the revolution in communication and information technologies."

Referring to this article, with which he completely agrees, Pierre Bellon puts the question,

"How can we reduce the threat from technocracy?"

And then he answers himself with force and conviction,

"We have to fight it vigorously, mobilizing the company at every level and get rid of everything which is superfluous. We must encourage intra-entrepreneurs as much as possible to

develop Sodexo. *That's the key to our growth. If we become a technocratic company with decisions made by people at the top who don't know the situation on the ground, it is finished, it will no longer have the spirit of entrepreneurship, there will be no more intra-entrepreneurs and that is how, by the way, companies fail. Then add the ego of those in charge and that's it, it's over. The internal brakes pre-empt any flexibility. To avoid the major risk of technocratic slide, you need to stand the pyramid on its head by giving more power and responsibility to the field staff while decentralizing to the maximum. Taking into account the importance of this word intra-entrepreneur, its definition is given in our general policy on human resources: the intra-entrepreneur is an executive who has full responsibility, i.e. they are charged with evaluating the potential for development in their entity, to satisfy the consumers and the clients better than their competitors, to have a better commercial performance than them, to manage more effectively, with lower operating and administrative costs than them, with the aim of increasing liquidity, operational results and sales turnover more quickly than them. A person in charge of motivating his teams and generally, developing the human resources in their entity. The true intra-entrepreneur is the one that delegates what exists and creates what does not.*

Consequently, as soon as each executive assumes their function, they must find one or more possible successors, give them additional responsibilities to test them and yield their position to them one day to take on other responsibilities in the Group. My dream since the start, has always been to become a large company of craftsmen endowed with responsibilities. And today I talk about intra-entrepreneurs. That's my conception of the company. I very quickly realized that, developing the company by myself, I would fail. As I had a certain idea of the development, I started to recruit women and men whom I considered to be better than me, or at least complementary to what I was. I said the same thing to them all—there are no career plans here. I will trust you; you will trust me and actually, you're the one who will make your own career plan. That is what happened. These women and men took on responsibilities in Marseilles, Bordeaux, Lyon and Paris, then later abroad, and they developed the company with me.

Sodexo has been a machine for manufacturing entrepreneurs. One should never forget the pioneering spirit right at the start of the venture—a mix of enthusiasm, versatility and audacity. I say it and I repeat it all the time. Internal promotion, that makes it possible for our executives and our people in charge to evolve, by entrusting them with more and more responsibilities, is the group's principal attraction. It's what the Anglo-Saxons call empowerment. It is the granting of more power to the people or the groups who want to affect the economic, social, political and ecological conditions that they experience. This is the managerial concept which must guide the transformation of Sodexo towards what I call a liberated company."

At 89 years of age, Pierre Bellon continues to think about the company, to defend his vision, with ardor and passion. In the pile of books on his desk, there is one which always remains on top. It is by Isaac Getz, who popularized the phrase 'liberated company' in 2009, in his book *'Freedom, Inc.: Free your employees and let them lead the company to higher productivity, profits and growth.'* Isaac Getz says,

"Too many people are stifled, hampered, opposed and paralyzed by bureaucracy and rules which do the opposite of helping them do their job to the best of their ability. These constraints give them the impression that they have no control over their professional life, which generates stress, tiredness and demotivation (…) All traditional companies must face a cost which never appears in the accounts—the cost of all that is not carried out because of the stifling effect of the technocratic chain. These costs are impossible to assess – the lost benefits, missed opportunities, creeping inefficiency (…) A liberated company trusts its employees and their know-how, by releasing their creativity and their spirit of initiative (…) The head of a company can never know everything that the least employee learns each day about the way the company operates and about its clients. Management theoreticians have borrowed a term from physics to describe the kind of information which the staff on the ground have. They talk about "weak signals." It is essential to detect these weak signals, which may be crucial one day."

Another reference book dear to Pierre Bellon, which cropped up in a number of our conversations, is the one by Pierre de Villiers 'What is a Boss?'

"*A true boss steers, without actually giving orders. They give the people concerned a clear and comprehensible overall vision, outline the global objective and the joint task to be done. They share the reasons for their choices and show people the problems to be solved. Then, they let the interested parties define the way to handle matters, each one at their own level, together with their colleagues, while respecting the aims and values of the organization (...) I believe that humor adds value to a boss. It is even an essential quality in my view because it helps inoculate you against stupidity, pushiness and pretension. What's more, humor distances you a bit from the events of daily life. It is an excellent cure for pride, which is one of the most dangerous afflictions for any man or woman. True greatness lies in simplicity and modesty.*"

To persuade *Sodexo* executives to question their behavior, their role, their way of managing, the company became one of the first in France to create a training center, the *Sodexo Management Institute* (*SMI*), conceived as a veritable school for intra-entrepreneurs.

*"Its purpose has always been to prepare
people's minds for change and for an international role, while contributing to the continuing
progress of executives. In a company like ours, it
is the women and men who make the difference.
They lie at the heart our competitive edge. It is
our duty to give them the tools which allow them
to develop and adapt their abilities in an
evolving world."*

As proof of the importance he places on
the *SMI*, Pierre Bellon has widely participated in many sessions, sharing his experiences, his ideas and answering questions.

*"It has given me a chance to talk about the
things I consider important: humility in the face
of the facts, broadmindedness, a sense of innova-
tion, the taste for risk, the permanent need to do
better, the ability to question yourself and to
adapt to changes, how to listen, care for
employees' wellbeing, the will to promote diversity, resistance to stress and a taste for optimism.
I have always pointed out that our priority must
be to remain true to the facts and what I call 'the
mirror.' There are several ways of looking at
oneself in a mirror. Some entrepreneurs bask in
their successes and those of their company; they*

are convinced that past successes are a guarantee of future ones. That is not our view. We, the executives of Sodexo, *must reinforce our strengths, but also constantly reduce our dysfunctions and our weaknesses. I often say that I have learned more from my failures than from our successes. In* Sodexo, *it is all right to make a mistake, provided you learn from it."*

CHAPTER 4

CAPITALISM

One of the important issues which has preoccupied the business world since 2018 is one of purpose. With this question at the heart of people's thinking: what is a company for? This issue became relevant partly due to the *Pacte* law (Action plan for the growth and the transformation of companies), put forward by Edouard Philippe's government. It establishes the possibility for a company to adopt a 'raison d'être,' or 'rationale,' making it possible to define a social responsibility that takes into account all its stakeholders. In other words, it is a question of redefining the role of the company in society. The issue is to take into account objectives other than profit alone and to escape the doctrines which hold that the company is directed in the exclusive interest of its shareholders, existing only for and through its stock exchange price. Naive? Utopian? Proof that this assertion gains a little traction every day came in January 2019 with a statement from Larry Fink, chairman of the largest asset managers in the world, exhorting companies to define... their 'raison d'être.' For *BlackRock*'s boss, manager of more than $6,000 billion worth of assets, a long-term view is essential. In 2018, the world's largest shareholder had already invited executives worldwide to work for the "*common good.*"

"*It has become paramount for companies that wish to attract and retain the best talents to clearly articulate their raison d'être. Millennials will occupy increasingly senior positions in companies. And 63% of Millennials think that the primary goal of companies should be 'to improve society and no longer to generate profit.'*"

"*Companies do not win in a world which loses,*" writes Patrick D' Humières, director of the *Académie Durable Internationale*, (Academy of International Sustainability) in his book '*La nature politique de l'entrepreneur' (The political nature of the entrepreneur)*." He analyzes the unprecedented changes which are driving companies to re-examine their societal contribution from top to bottom.

"We are experiencing an undeniable and incontrovertible systemic transition. The first challenge is that of the climate and global sustainability, compounded by a numerical-societal change triggered by global digitalization and accelerated by the millennial generation, in a context of growing geopolitical instability. So many ruptures, revolutions and disruptions which are shattering the old world of the 20th century and inaugurating a period in which each person has a share in the responsibility to avoid the worst and, most importantly, to build the best (...). Faced with shouldering these gigantic and inevitable challenges, the emergence of solutions equal to the task cannot be and will not be achievable without the involvement of businesses, taking into account their activities' impact on the planet and on people's lives. We are entering an age of an inextricable global connection between society and business, obliging the latter to integrate societal implications upstream of decisions, of their own volition, leading to choices no longer solely guided by their primary interests."

The 'raison d'être' is at the heart of all that Pierre Bellon does, both within *Sodexo* but also externally, because of his involvement in foundations and associations which he has created or in which he participates, and his responsibilities within the sphere of employers, where he has been enormously proactive.

"I've spent two thirds of my time outside my company. It has broadened my mind." Everything started with his membership in the Marseilles section of the *CJP* of which he was president in 1963 and 1964, before having to fight at national level against the disappearance of this movement which brought him so much. In 1968, there was a troubled period of immense political, social and cultural upheaval sparked by an unprecedented crisis in France. The *CJP* interpretation of these events was condemned by the *CNPF* of the time, because the former considered that the explosive situation resulted from the bankruptcy of traditional management as defended by business leaders.

"Their [the business leaders'] attitude choked the search for company reform through evasiveness" wrote Beatrice Touchelay, in an article entitled *"French employers and the division of power in the company between 1946 and 1968."*

In other words, the *CJP*, despite very many publications, interventions and statements, failed to soften the conservative ideas of employers. In this quarrel between the 'old hands' and the 'modern ones,' the question of the impotence of the movement in which Pierre Bellon participated was posed, in particular by one of those emblematic figures, José Bidegain, former president from 1961 to 1964, who esteemed that the *Centre des Jeunes Patrons* (*CJP*—Center for Young Owners) had had its day. He argued for winding it up on the pretext that, going forward, it would be preferable to limit the ranks of the employers to the executives of large companies alone.

"He betrayed us. My attachment to the CJP *was too important to let to him do that. Personally, I wanted to safeguard the movement. I said to José that unlike him, I continued to believe in the utility of a structure made up of small and*

medium companies, generally in the hands of owners under 45 years old. As my buddy Bernard Lecat, born in Marseilles like me, then president of the CJD, had just thrown in the towel, nauseated by the turn matters had taken, there was no choice but to tackle the national presidency to ensure its survival."

The first decision was to change the name. The *CJP* became the *Centre des Jeunes Dirigeants* (*CJD* – Center for Young Executives), to underline its members' function as management rather than as owners.

The organization's Congress was held September 26-28, 1968 in La Baule. In his introductory statement, Pierre Bellon described his vision for a company.

"France has been shaken by the serious events of these last months. The unexpected revolt of the students spread at an extraordinary speed throughout the country. Alongside demands for better working conditions, higher wages, greater job security and opportunities for young people, this movement translated much higher aspirations: for men to be treated like men, treated with dignity, not to be reduced to the level of a thing, but to have their ability to assume responsibility

recognized together with their ability to take the initiative in society's organization, whether in a company, university, or society. (…)

Faced with the occupation of universities and factories, citizens have been in fear of civil war. Business leaders wanted work to restart, knowing that one month from the beginning of the Common Market, a long strike would seriously destabilize the French economy. But we young employers, hungry for progress and renewal, have felt close to the demands of the students and workers. Harmonious economic growth, more fairly distributed, and a society managed at all levels by responsible men, are slogans which we understand well. Finding ways to translate these slogans into reality, is to try to transform economic growth into development (…).

What is the development of our companies for? What use is economic progress if accompanied by social crises, if used to further enrich the wealthy, to impoverish the poorest, if accompanied by under-employment and permanent unemployment, if it imposes the current dramatic geographical and professional mobility, if it contributes to the decline of certain regions, if it allows, despite everything, the spread of hunger in the world? These are the questions public opinion is asking of us, we, the people in charge of companies. We cannot run away. This is the true extent of our responsibility (…).

The effectiveness of the company boss is all the greater if it is based on trust in men (…). We have to realize that the most sustainable way to succeed is for a company to consider the men who constitute it as its best capital (…). The devolution of power has as its fundamental principle that the best equipped man to make the decision, when he is well informed, is the one closest to the facts.

This means that owner bosses accept an ultimate and voluntary limit to their omnipotence. This means that we agree to recognize that people have the right to make mistakes. This means that it is necessary that, within the company, the rules of the game are such that several people have the courage to tell you what they think of you and of your decisions (…). Collegiate management is more demanding than any other for the participants as regards their behavior and their competence. It should also pay off, because the influence of people in the company who express themselves freely, is clearly a dynamizing element compared to traditionally structured companies. This is a hot topic because in some respect it calls into question authority and management in the company. And as you know, in the eyes of traditional employers tackling this problem is tantamount to revolution."

Pierre Bellon, denouncing a capitalism which sets people in opposition to one another and pleading for a capitalism of reconciliation. This 'disruptive' speech was made four years before that of Antoine Riboud, owner founder of *Danone*, given in Marseilles on October 25, 1972, at the *CNPF* national convention. The latter, under the title "*Growth and quality of life,*" is more often referred to, but it only follows in the footsteps of the founder of *Sodexo*, echoing Pierre Bellon's engagement.

"*Economic growth and the market economy have transformed and shaken up the standard of living in the Western world. It is indisputable. But the result is far from perfect (...). This growth has often sacrificed the environment and working conditions to economic efficiency. This is why people decry it, and even reject it, as the*

end of the industrial age. Letting it go on; contin-
uing to trust in the Laws of Chance would lead
us inevitably to Revolution."

When we read these views, putting the company at the service of human development, we may well wonder how we've gone from May '68 to the current Yellow Jackets crisis, born of a deep sense of social and fiscal injustice. What did we miss? You might well ask. How could the capitalism of these last fifty years turn its back to this extent on what might be called a 'raison d'être,' focused on 'the common good.'

"Capitalism is there to make it possible for entrepreneurs to carry out their projects, to create wealth and employment. That's all."

Except that this has been perverted by the devastation wrought by hyper-financialization of the economy. Which means that companies live under the dictatorship of the financial markets and their short termism.

"This system in which investors are shareholders for only a few months, a few weeks or a few days, leads to a capitalism which no longer exists. If it is a question of enriching a few people, speculators, who couldn't care less about others, well, I am completely against this type of capitalism."

Is it inevitable? Pierre Bellon has no qualms in saying that he is a capitalist, a liberal, and against all state intervention. He believes in the market economy, despite its crudeness and shortfalls. He's familiar with the brutality and bitterness of competition, which is always fierce. All his life, he has faced setbacks, and defended himself too. It's fair game, both in victory and defeat. But what he can't accept or bear are the low blows. And he knows, from experience, what he's talking about.

In 1980, Pierre Bellon was betrayed by a bank and his principal ally in the battle for the acquisition of *Jacques Borel International*. At the time the company was in great difficulty, in the hands of speculators following the departure of its founder. A scenario entailing asset stripping by shareholders, more interested in a logic of speculation than by the wish to successfully complete an entrepreneurial project, seemed to be holding sway. Hence Pierre Bellon's opposition to this project and his interest in this target operating in two of the same sectors as *Sodexo*: collective food services and luncheon vouchers. But he was not the only one throwing his hat in the ring. Competing with him were Paul Dubrule and Gerard Pélisson, two great entrepreneurs, founders of the *Novotel* chain of hotels in 1967. The confrontation turned into a stock exchange battle in which *Sodexo* found a heavyweight ally, the distribution group *Codec-Una*. Together, they had a good chance of winning. Except that at the last minute, *Codec-Una* decided to throw its equity behind *Novotel*, in violation of the agreement with *Sodexo*, on the advice of the financial intermediary who changed sides "*against the promise of a better commission*" as *L'Express* magazine reported at the time.

"*I was betrayed by a banker,*" Pierre Bellon still broods, finding in this yet another argument for mistrusting financiers. Subsequent defeat became inevitable, allowing the *Novotel-JBI* merger to give rise to the *Accor Group*.

However, Pierre Bellon had not finished with the Dubrule—Pélisson duo and he would face them once again at the end of the 1980s over the acquisition of the *Compagnie*

Internationale des Wagons-Lits et du Tourisme (*CIWLT*). Unfortunately for the founder of *Sodexo*, history repeated itself and *Accor* ended by snatching the business from under his nose, helped again by a financier, Albert Frère, who sold his participation in *Générale de Belgique*, the Trojan horse for the Dubrule-Pelisson pair.

"I made a major mistake. I did not understand that Frère was a speculator. When he went into a business, he was merely waiting to get out. Me, I am an entrepreneur. A company's purpose is to progress."

Pierre Bellon has no problem with capitalism, a system which affords an infinite capacity for movement and renewal and has a formidable creative force. For him, as for a very great silent majority of honest and virtuous owners, a market society does not necessarily hold the seeds of a destructive fascination with money, the money which makes people crazy and which corrupts everything. In 2010, the Nobel Prizewinner for Economics, Joseph Stiglitz, named the evil which is the canker of capitalism in a book with the explicit title: "Age of Greed:

Triumph of Finance..." 'Greed' is exactly the word which Pierre Bellon employs when reminded of the scandal which touched Richard Grasso, the president of the New York Stock Exchange (NYSE) at the beginning of the 2000s. The two men know each other because that was the period that *Sodexo* entered on the *New York Stock Exchange*.

"I made the silly mistake of thinking that being on Wall Street would make it easier for Sodexo *employees working in the United States to buy shares in our company. But as, in fact, one can acquire them without much difficulty on any money market, this quotation was pointless. Except that it meant I met Richard Grasso. At the time of our quotation, I gave him a beautiful miniature sports car because he loved cars."*

It was a gift that Pierre Bellon would soon regret. At the end of November 2003 came the first revelations about Richard Grasso having received exorbitant bonuses of $190 million, causing one of the most serious crises in the history of the *NYSE,* involving the downfall of its chairman and CEO.

"When I saw that, I said myself that with deviancy and excesses like that, capitalism is finished."

In his stand against capitalism run amok, Pierre Bellon also has in his sights the banks accused of irresponsibility at the time of the world banking crisis of 2008, caused by the subprime disaster in the United States.

"The fact that bank executives agreed mortgages for completely insolvent private individuals is absolutely scandalous. All the banks were implicated."

Most scandalous of all, however, is that since this incendiary bomb which plunged the world into economic chaos with dramatic social consequences, the misdemeanors of the banks are far from having been eradicated. A report from the *Boston Consulting Group* (*BCG*) reveals that the total sum of fines paid by the banking houses of the world, since 2009, has reached the astronomical sum of €332 billion (27 billion in 2018 alone, against 22 billion one year earlier).

"When you look at tax havens, all the banks say, 'it's not me.' But you just have to press a button and all the names appear one after another," adds Pierre Bellon, in reference to the scandal of the Paradise Papers which revealed the extent of global offshore financing.

"It is nevertheless incredible that the banks are still first in line when it comes to thinking of reforms to make companies more ethical, whereas they are simultaneously working on increasingly sophisticated ways to help their clients defraud the tax authorities. I've been wary of bankers for a very long time. In 1973, Sodexo launched itself on public markets and needed money. In response to a request for liquidity, the banking institutions turned them down. It was ridiculous. During the whole period when our accounts were in the black, the bankers tried to persuade me to borrow. And the day when I needed money, credit was completely blocked. It nearly finished us. I decided never to depend in the short term on the banks again."

CHAPTER 5

INDEPENDENCE

Sodexo is unlike any other private company, because the Bellon family still holds more than a majority of the voting rights, through *Bellon SA* holdings, owner of 42,2 % of the equity. Within *Bellon SA*, Pierre, his wife and four children hold over three-quarter of the shares, which ensures them total control of the company, founded in 1966. This completely protects *Sodexo* from falling prey to predatory or ill-disposed speculators, at a time when shareholder activists—known as 'vulture funds' have never been more rapacious for companies.

"This new-kind of raider descends without warning on the share capital of large groups, demanding strategic change, or massive econo-mies, or better governance. And even if they do not always achieve their aims, they send shock

waves through the organization, putting pressure on executives and administrators," wrote Guillaume Maujean in *Les Echos,* February 19, 2019.

These activists' methods and objectives are very strongly criticized because they are seen as the worst type of investor, having considerable financial fire power, but godless and lawless, ready for anything to achieve their objective. This is to force up the share price as much as possible within the shortest possible time. In 2018, 226 companies across the globe were targeted, as against 188 a year earlier, according to a study undertaken by *Lazard.* More than half of these attacks affected American groups. But now there's a new phenomenon—Europe and France, spared until now, are the fresh hunting grounds for these vulture funds. Proof of this is the surprise attack from the most dreaded hedge fund in the world, *Elliott Management,* on *Pernod Ricard,* to the general stupefaction of the company and the Paris stock exchange. This time, it was a family company, like *Sodexo,* which was targeted, except that in the case of the world number two in wines and spirits the Ricard family itself no longer holds half of the voting rights. It holds approximately 15% of the equity. Which makes all the difference under the circumstances. The chairman and CEO of the group, Alexandre Ricard, has had no other choice but to report on results and corporate governance to this hedge fund, even though it only has a 2.5% shareholding. But it also has such a large war chest that it could start to seriously undermine and desta-bilize, in an effort to rally sufficient share-holders to the cause of strategy change in one of the jewels in the crown of French industry. It doesn't seem possible. However, governed by the lure of short-term profit, modern capitalism, in the hands of unscrupulous shareholders, permits this astonishing kind of situation which may trigger very heavy social and human consequences in the event of lay-offs and decommissioning.

In this context, as rogue as it is brutal, the convention signed on May 22, 2008 by Pierre Bellon, his wife and their four chil-dren, is an act which one could almost qualify as 'political.' They committed them-selves, their grandchildren and direct descendants, not to sell any shares in *Bellon SA* holdings outside the family group, comprising direct heirs to the owner-founder, for the next fifty years.

"This convention protects Sodexo's independence completely, as desired by all the employees. It's a safeguard which prevents the company from falling into the hands of a financial or industrial group. Which other company in the world with Sodexo's *global dimension can pride itself on such a long-lasting engagement?* Sodexo *is an independent company.* Sodexo *is a family company. It will remain one. And if you ask me, for how long? My answer is—forever."*

This independence is a precious guarantee that they can continue to build. Pierre Bellon is a 'builder.' In 1987, he wrote a letter to his children full of integrity and unsettling honesty, full of emotion. *Sodexo*'s founder opens up as in no other document. It is an intimate confession which questions the very nature of the entrepreneur.

"'I founded and developed Sodexo because I wanted to do something on my own account and needed to fulfil my dream and spread my

wings. Heading up a company, making it progress and grow, requires permanent effort researching and developing, which I love, even if sometimes the knocks, failures and challenges are discouraging. To each, his own. My strength is in entrepreneurship. I practice my trade as head of a company like a mission. I aim to satisfy clients, respond to the needs of staff, make a profit for shareholders. But in developing the company, I have become very rich. In 1966 shares in Sodexo were worth almost nothing. Today, they have a very high value. I also enriched my sisters, my brother and you, since you are my heirs.

A large fortune gives you a secure, more convenient, more agreeable life, but I consider it more of a bad than a good thing. Love, friendship, courage, loyalty, respect for your engagements, devotion, generosity, honesty, work, respect and consideration for others, the quest for an ideal, are, for me, the only essential values. I am sure that they will also be yours. The money is without value. In my view, it even represents a serious threat to those who become attached to it. Look around you—so many families are at each other's throats over money—it's dreadful!

Like me, you know people who despise others, because they have money, which they have usually inherited. You know that the motivation to work is all too easily removed by having money.

Everyone needs to fulfil their dreams, nobody can do that for you, even less can it be bought. To be fulfilled, you yourself need to have achieved something, to love and be loved, to start a family, to raise children, to be active in an association, to be interested in art, to create, to lead. There are many ways. Mom and I will be able to help you, but it is for you, to find your path and your purpose in the course of your lives. I did not seek to become rich, nor did you, but it is something I need to speak to you about today. My fortune is mainly made up of Sodexo *shares. Some already belong to you because I donated them to you, the remainder will come to you on my death. To be a shareholder brings advantages: for example, if the company does well, the shareholder receives dividends each year. But it also brings responsibilities. You hold voting rights at Shareholder meetings and therefore the power to make decisions, crucial to the survival and development of the company. In your case, your power, your responsibilities and therefore your duties, are all the more important as you will hold the majority of* Sodexo *shares.* Sodexo *is one of my reasons for living. I hope that you accept the same rules as those which I have imposed on myself as a shareholder, which are the following.*

The interests of the Sodexo *group, that is those of the clients, the employees and the minority shareholders take priority over yours.* Sodexo *must remain a group independent of other industrial and financial groups. That means that you should be united and that you cannot freely dispose of your shares. The executives of the* Sodexo *group, if they are to develop, must be selected from among the most competent. Your positions as major shareholders give neither to you, nor to any member of your family, the right to run* Sodexo. *If your ambition is to take a senior position in the Group, you may, on three conditions: you follow normal promotion procedures, you demonstrate competence and you are co-opted by the management in place."*

The appointment of Sophie Bellon in 2016 as chairwoman to the *Sodexo* board of directors, in place of her father, must be viewed in the light of the principles recorded in this letter. The story of this transfer of power began five years earlier, when Pierre Bellon brought together his four children to announce that he wished to see one of them succeeding him but that he didn't expect to choose, in accordance with his desire not to confuse the family tree and the company organigram.

"My children have been administrators of Sodexo *almost since they reached the age of the majority. I told them that given that they control* Sodexo, *one of them would take over from me. And I added that on no account would I make the choice. At that time, except for Astrid, my youngest daughter, who was advancing in the world of audio-visual production, my three other children, Sophie, Nathalie and François-Xavier had all grown with the company. They all worked there at one time or another. With a very clear rule that I had fixed from the start that my children would be co-opted by the hierarchy and that their positions as shareholders would not give them any rights. They all three decided to stand as a candidate for my succession.*

When I say that I have enormous admiration for my children, it is because they put ambition for the company and development of the group before their personal ambition, which is in my opinion utterly remarkable on their part. That is due as well to the way in which my wife and I raised them. It's extremely important and I'll admit I'm very proud of it. By mutual agreement, my children decided to go and see four administrators who knew them all very well and ask them to choose between them. My children were at their disposal if they wanted to find out more about them. Then my children added another condition to this selection process—they did not want any explanations justifying the eventual selection. In the end, in February 2013 my daughter Sophie was unanimously chosen. Nathalie remained at her post as CEO of Sodexo *Sports and Leisure and my two other children kept their responsibilities within* Bellon SA. "

Three years later, on January 26, 2016, the great day came for passing the baton from father to eldest daughter. The ceremony took place in prestigious surroundings at the *Pré Catelan*, of three Michelin star fame, whose owner since 2011 has been none other than *Sodexo*. That day, shareholders were invited to a general assembly with strong emotional undercurrents. It is an understatement to say that a page was turned at *Sodexo*, for even if Pierre Bellon remained Honorary Chairman of the company which he had founded exactly 50 years previously, his last appearance on stage as a Chairman of the Board without doubt constituted an historical landmark in the life of the group. On the platform, he introduced his daughter Sophie as,

"A rigorous, courageous and generous woman totally committed to diversity (…) The board of directors is convinced that she will make an excellent chairwoman for Sodexo."

CHAPTER 6

SERVICES

At the heart of the business leaders' establishment, Pierre Bellon was initially one of the vice-presidents of the *CNPF*, then of the *Medef*. Over the years, this has made him a leading figure in the organization. But less known, if at all, is the role of dissenter he played behind the scenes, opposing, sometimes singlehandedly, a movement which always favored industry and neglected service to others. However, recognizing the value of services has always been his political battleground. He counters his detractors with,

"Industry destroys jobs, services create them," which is what Sodexo does.

In the 1970s, it happened that he worked with Jacques Ferry, president of the *Iron and Steel Industry Group*, an honorable man and a

very influential figure within the *Conseil éco-
nomique et social* (*CES*—Social and
Economic Council). However, the French
iron and steel industry was already in crisis,
quasi-bankrupt even, causing the closure of
many factories in the Lorraine basin.

*"What was my connection with him? None.
I was creating jobs with my company and he was
in a sector which was laying people off. I felt very
uncomfortable in this grouping of private companies. I was practically always in disagreement
with the decisions which were made. So, generally, I did not vote with them."*

Leaving the *CES* in 1976, Pierre Bellon
uttered this lucid but damning comment,
"Looking back, I was only 5% effective."

Pierre Bellon would often be in the
minority in his vigorous criticism of the executive policy within the employers' organization, whether the *CNPF* or the *Medef.*

*"I had my reputation. I've always been inde-
pendent. I say what I think. I'm a damn
nuisance. So, I spent my time saying how things
were, and generally in opposition to others. On
several occasions, I said to the various presidents
that we were wasting our time. I told Ernest*

Antoine Seillière, president of the Medef *from 1997 to 2005, that we'd failed completely. When you see what's happening today, it just shows how useless we were. I take my share of responsibility. We didn't change French society or modernize the relationship with trade unions. I dreamed of a strong trade unionism in France. It has never existed. That's why things are happening as they are today."*

Pierre Bellon, *enfant terrible* among employers. Unsurprising perhaps when the *CJD* had been under the sway of the very powerful *Union des Industries et métiers de la métallurgie* (the *UIMM* – the Union of Metallurgy trades and Industry) for decades, as Claire Guélaud wrote on October 10, 2007, in an article in *Le Monde* entitled: '*The steel heart of employers.*'

"For over 106 years, this subsidiary of the Comité des forges (The Forging Mills' Committee), as well-versed in the class struggle as the CGT (Confédération Générale du Travail—General Workers' Union), had long been the owners and business leader's suggestion box. It made kings of them. It spread its network throughout the world of politics, trade-unions

and the higher echelons of the civil service. It fashioned the social doctrines of the CNPF *for more than half a century. It was involved in all the employers' struggles, making it a point of honor to defend to the end the interests of its constituents, whom it equated to the elite of French industry. And too bad for the other employers' federations, services first and foremost."*

Still today, the *UIMM* remains one of the most powerful components of the *Medef*, together with the Banking and Insurance Federations. However, for Pierre Bellon, this triumvirate, even taking into account its relative importance to the economy, cannot claim to speak for all branches of industry, even if it thinks it has a right to.

"I observed that the richer a sector was amongst the business leaders and owners, the fewer jobs it created."

Faced with this body of business leaders and owners which did not sufficiently defend the interests of service firms, in 1979 Pierre Bellon created, within the *CNPF*, the *Comité de Liaisons des Professions de Services* (*CLS* – Committee for Liaising between Service

Professions), which in 2003 became *Groupement des Professions de Services* (*GPS*—the Group for Service Professions).

"I feel passionate about the service industry. I've devoted much time to it. Those are my roots. Our family company was about service, not industry. When I founded Sodexo, *services were looked down on, the undervalued sector of company food services was belittled. It was the poor relative of the economy. When I arrived in Paris, people looked down on me utterly. One, because I was from Marseilles. And two, because my trade was not well regarded. This is why that I wanted to raise the standing of this sector and give to our employees a sense of pride in their trade."*

"Outside my company, I never ceased to plead the cause of services. In 1978, I contributed to the first large scale document on the subject. It was a report on 'Employment in the tertiary sector' *published by the* CES. *I was supported by certain people from* INSEE *(French national institute for statistical and economic studies) who were convinced of the importance of the service industries. We clearly pointed out, using precise figures, the fall of manpower in industry and*

public works, and we stressed that during the previous fifteen years, three-quarters of the jobs created in France had been in the service sector. We also indicated that over the coming years the tertiary sector in France would become the main source of new employment. But today, forty years later, we are still not listened to. That's why I continue to repeat again and again that France must adopt a proper strategy for the service industries, because services make a major contribution, just as much as industry, to the competitiveness of the French economy. Since 1958, they have generated 85% of French growth and all of net job creation. The service's landscape in France will radically change in the next ten years, as a result of five major changes: an explosion in world trade thanks to the digital revolution, the demand from emergent countries, deregulation, the consolidation of competition and the explosion in trading (more than 50% of world trade will be carried out in the service sector, as against 20% in 2011). It is imperative to understand which services have the greatest potential for creating value and for employment. They are in software, media, the Internet, data processing departments, cultural goods, personal and residential services, care services, nurseries, medical research, tourism etc."

"How it is that the authorities had a policy for agriculture, a policy for industry and have never been truly interested in services? It should be said that a few years ago, certain apparatchiks representing industry, manifested an arrogance and condescension bordering on contempt towards creators, commercial entrepreneurs, the distribution and service industries. They asserted that the tertiary sector was unproductive and was not faced with international competition. The power of industry in the business leaders and owners' establishment structures did not help us get across to the authorities the importance of the tertiary sector. We were being completely discriminated against. There was no access to research, no export aid, no financing for immaterial assets… and unfortunately contrary to many other OECD countries, we have never had a proper strategy in France for promoting private service companies. For this reason, during my many years with the CNPF, I was very often completely at odds with others on this subject."

"I never walked away because how would it have helped if I'd resigned? Not at all. And

I was not going to create a second employers' group, so I made do with the existing structures. But all the same, in spite of the reservations of the CNPF *council, in 1987 I created the* Association pour le Progrès du Management *(APM—Association for the Progress of Management), because my experience was that we never discussed enterprises as enterprises. From the start, my aim was to take the enterprise leaders out of their isolation to exchange ideas with their peers. The idea was simple: to help companies progress, you have to help their bosses progress. The* APM *is an opportunity to tackle subjects common to the bosses, in complete confidentiality. With the humanistic values which have brought us together, such as respect of the person and open-mindedness. Through these exchanges, we seek to better grasp the complexity of the world. The association numbers more than 7600 bosses, divided into 370 clubs in about thirty different countries. There are 350 experts from every field to open the eyes of company leaders. Through this I have been able to form opinions on a number of subjects, which I would never have done if I had not taken part in movements such as this. I am very proud of the utility of the* APM. *"*

Conclusion

HUMAN DEVELOPMENT

Monday March 11, 2019. My collaboration with Pierre Bellon on this book was reaching its end. Final conversations, last corrections. I saw him at his office, as before. That day, he invited me to a *Stop Hunger* evening, being held the following Wednesday at the Seine Musicale music complex in Boulogne Billancourt. This humanitarian organization was formed over 20 years ago by *Sodexo* employees in Boston USA, to fight against hunger and help those suffering from it. The March 13 evening consisted in collecting donations around a dinner put together by the Michelin starred chefs, Thierry Marx and Frederic Anton. Pierre Bellon was in the forefront, a supporter of *Stop Hunger* from its outset.

"Hunger is not inevitable. Sodexo *is continuously fighting against food wastage and has*

always wanted to spread the hope of a quality of life for all, so this engagement is natural. We have more than 40,000 employees who are involved in this humanitarian cause, their families too sometimes, and the same goes for some of our millions of consumers, our thousands of clients, suppliers, and shareholders. "

The former 1954 *HEC* graduate, Pierre Bellon, is also involved in this major business school's Foundation, supporting scholarships assessed on social criteria. This benefits approximately a fifth of the students. And then, above all, *Sodexo*'s founder has created his own foundation devoted to human development, which works with people in difficulty in France and abroad, especially young people and their families, in three areas—fulfilment of human potential, work life and literacy.

Before I left Pierre Bellon's office, he laid down one last condition for the publication of this book.

"The people in Sodexo *must feel proud of it because as I've often said, we have built this company together. I'd like to thank all those who have taken part in this adventure with me.*

My comrades along the way, the CEOs, site managers and the thousands of women and men who, carry out our mission every day on the ground, improving the quality of daily life. I also hope that this book will serve to tell my children and my family about what I've done."

This reminded me of an extract from his speech made on the occasion of the presentation of the *Légion d'honneur* to his eldest daughter Sophie, in March 2016. He spoke of his wife Danielle, who worked for the accomplishment of this book project from its inception.

"Nani, I was often absent. You raised our children beautifully, with love, intelligence and good sense. You did everything to make our home pleasant, welcoming, warm and merry whether in Marseilles, Paris, Cassis, La Bédoule or Pra-Loup. Thank you. You also helped me in Sodexo's *geographical development, whether in the Benelux countries, in Spain, in Italy, in Russia, in the Middle East, in the Far East or in Latin America. When I was going to visit French companies working in these distant regions, I asked you to mingle with the people living there so as to better understand their ways*

of life, their purchasing power, their means of transport, their culture and their religion, which helped me a lot in the international development of Sodexo. All that I have undertaken in my life, I owe to you."

Pierre Bellon is a reserved man. But he can open up, nonetheless. Grateful. Endearing. He always puts people first. And humanity, the underlying theme of this book to the very end, is at the heart of one of the major issues for our societies today: coexistence, threatened by social dislocation and territorial divide. That's why it carries a useful message. Important. Because there is one fact that will affect us all—the world which is taking shape will not progress through more artificial intelligence, robotization and digital technology alone. Without doubt, the new technologies hold solutions for improving people's lives and helping solve huge problems like climate change, so long as they are put to good use. But it is obvious that, faced with the danger of dehumanization and its devastating effects, already visible, the best way to fight it is to put humanity back at the heart of each project. Entrepreneurial or political. While investing in trust and the delegation of responsibilities to those on the ground. Society needs us to take more and better care of people. First and foremost, of those who are fragile, alone, old and dependent. This can be achieved through more mutual aid and through listening. And services. This is where *Sodexo*, founded over fifty years ago, more than ever today finds its whole 'raison d'être.' Working for a better quality of life. It has never been so urgently needed. To accomplish this, the structure built by its founder is a formidable heritage for his daughter Sophie, heading up the board of directors. And for its 460,000 employees. The nobility of their mission is their greatest pride. And the greatest of rewards for Pierre Bellon.

TABLE OF CONTENTS

Ce volume a été mis en pages
par Pixellence
59100 Roubaix

Ce volume,
le cinquantième
de la collection « Entreprises et société »
publié aux Éditions Les Belles Lettres
a été achevé d'imprimer
en octobre 2019
sur les presses de
l'imprimerie Jouve

N° d'éditeur : 9466
N° d'imprimeur : 2909348S